Aboriginal Global Pioneers
Book 2

Australian Aboriginal Trade

Sharing Goods and Services

Marji Hill

Published by The Prison Tree Press 2024
Copyright © 2024 Marji Hill

The Prison Tree Press
Suite 124
1-10 Albert Avenue
Broadbeach, Queensland 4218
https://marjihill.com
https://www.fastselfpublishing.com

Disclaimer:
All the material contained in this book is provided for educational and informational purposes only. No responsibility can be taken for any results or outcomes resulting from the use of this material.

While every care has been taken to trace and acknowledge copyright the publishers tender their apologies for any accidental infringement where copyright has proved untraceable.

Every attempt has been made to provide information that is both accurate and effective, however, the author does not assume any responsibility for the accuracy or use/misuse of this information.

Acknowledgement is given to Canva for most of the illustrations in this book.

A catalogue record for this work is available from the National Library of Australia

Aboriginal Global Pioneers (Series of 5 Books)

Australian Aboriginal Origins: Earliest Beginnings (Book 1)
Australian Aboriginal Trade: Sharing Goods and Services (Book 2)
Australian Aboriginal Religion: Country and Dreaming (Book 3)
Australian Aboriginal Fire: Managing Country (Book 4)
Australian Aboriginal Medicine: Caring for People (Book 5)

ISBN 978-0-9756571-4-0 Hardback
ISBN 978-0-9756571-5-7 eBook

Australian Non-Fiction | First Nations | History

Acknowledgements

I acknowledge the Traditional Custodians of Country
throughout Australia
and their connections to land, sea, and community.

I pay my respect to elders, past, present, and emerging
and extend my respect to all First Nations peoples today.

In the spirit of reconciliation,
my mission is to increase understanding
between the First Nations and other Australians
and to provide people from all over the globe
some basic understanding of Australia's first people,
their history, and cultures.

Marji Hill

Contents

INTRODUCTION

Australia's First Nations people were global pioneers in many ways. Not only were they among the first great sea voyagers, First Nations people were global pioneers in religion, art, aerodynamics, technology, land management, medicine and commerce.

Before 1788, First Nations people had an elaborate system of trade throughout the continent.

There were traditional trading pathways. Goods moved across the continent from north to south and from east to west.

It was not only goods that travelled. Trade items included songs, ceremonies, ideas and these travelled along with things like pituri, ochre, tools, and ornaments.

Trade went on in Australia for many thousands of years. While Europe and Asia had the Silk Road and Spice Trade, First Nations people had their overland trading pathways.

These trading routes connected First Nations people throughout the country including people from the Torres Strait and Papua New Guinea.

Not only did First Nations people have trade connections that crisscrossed the continent, there were international trade connections as well. First Nations people were part of trade relationships with people of Southeast Asia and China.

This was long before the British ever occupied Australia. A trade route linked the northern shores of Australia to Asia across the ocean.

The movement of goods across the continent and beyond highlights the creativity and industriousness of First Nations people. They were involved in commerce for thousands of years.

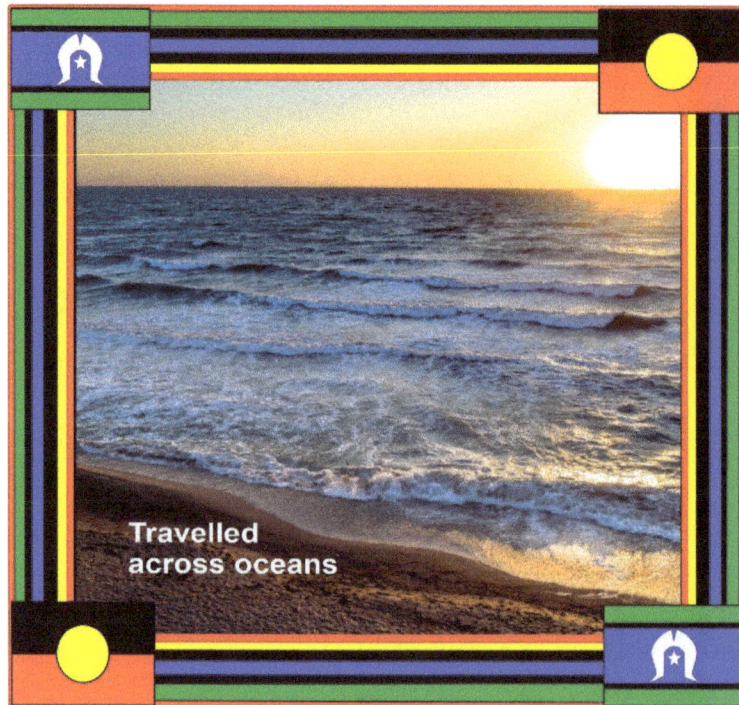

An Australia to Asia trans-ocean trade route existed

As you begin to understand the nature of First Nations commerce, you will gain an appreciation for the ingenuity and adaptability of Australia's First Nations people and their lasting impact on this continent's history.

PATHWAYS

First Nations Australians were great traders. If they lacked something they needed they got it from somewhere else. If goods such as stone, ochre, tools, or other items were not normally available to a group they acquired them through trade.

Trade allowed people to improve the quality of their lives in the same way as international trade helps people today.

Trading pathways went across the Australian continent. This meant trade routes crossed country which was owned by different First Nations groups.

People were safe to travel, provided they remained on the defined trading routes and did not do anything to offend those whose country they passed through.

This was essential to ensure safe travel across territories owned by various groups. Travelling these trading corridors required an intricate understanding of the land, its resources, and the social agreements between different groups.

The routes were carefully managed to avoid conflict. They were often marked by natural features like rivers, mountains, or trees.

Traders would perform rituals and exchange gifts to gain passage through another group's territory, fostering mutual respect and cooperation.

This system of trade routes created a network of connected communities, each contributing to and benefiting from the broader economic and cultural exchanges.

People travelled long distances to trade and to get the goods they wanted. One trader might set before him an elaborate set of carved and decorated boomerangs while another might offer a bag of pituri.

RELATIONSHIPS

Trade fostered relationships between neighbouring groups. People came to know their trading partners and to respect them in their dealings.

These markets were also an effective way of settling disputes between antagonistic groups because the exchange of gifts was often more acceptable than fighting.

People came to know and understand each other better by exchanging cultural items and special knowledge. They learned to respect each other's cultural differences and religious traditions.

FIRST EVIDENCE OF TRADE

At the burial sites at Lake Mungo in southwestern New South Wales, the skeletons of a man and a woman were found stained with red ochre. Archaeological evidence tells us that these remains were buried over 40,000 years ago.

Lake Mungo

Ochre and man-made tools were also found in the area. As ochre cannot be found anywhere near Lake Mungo, it must have been brought in from another region.

Not only does the ochre provide evidence for the practice of religious ritual all that time ago but also it shows that people had begun to trade, often over long distances, scarce materials that were highly valued.

People began trading when they had a surplus of goods which were scarce in other places and which people wanted.

At Parachilna in South Australia, for example, there is a large deposit of red ochre which was sought after for ceremonies. Blocks of this ochre were traded to people who lived as far away as North Queensland, Victoria and southern New South Wales.

Red Ochre

Other goods, such as pearl shells and boomerangs were also bartered over long distances. Shell from Papua New Guinea even got to western New South Wales.

It was not only goods that travelled vast distances. Some people, like the Dieri in South Australia, visited places hundreds of kilometres away.

EXCHANGE

Money was not used for trading goods. Instead, they were exchanged for something of value.

There is evidence, for example, that people travelled more than 100 kilometres to a quarry at Mount William in Victoria to obtain shards of axe-stone. Once an exchange was negotiated, a customer could use that stone to further negotiate business with another person. That person, in turn, would continue the process with other trading partners.

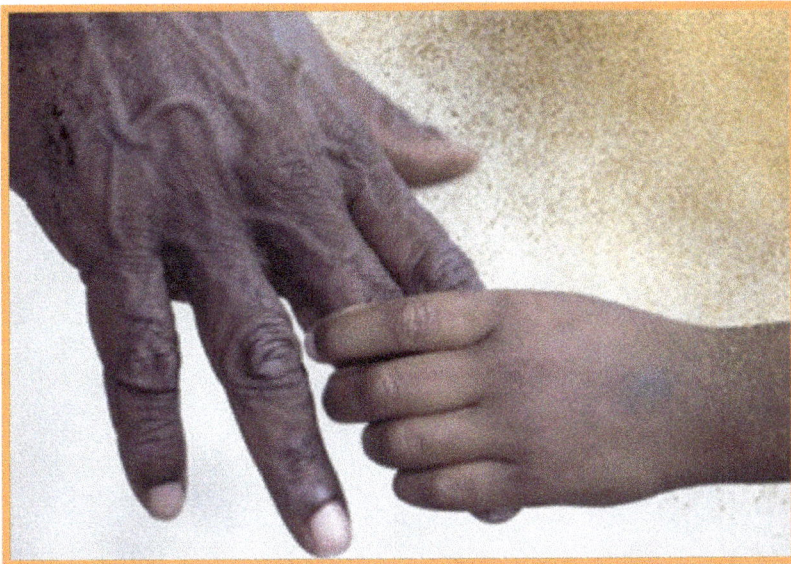

Trading partners

Another example is that reed spear shafts from Swan Hill on the Murray River, 300 kilometres from Mount William, were exchanged for the hard, tough volcanic greenstone from the quarry.

In other cases, the greenstone was exchanged for sandstone from the St Kilda area in Melbourne.

The movement of tools, such as axes made from high-quality stone found in specific regions, demonstrated the specialised knowledge and skills each group possessed, which were then shared through trade.

DEFINED TRADE ROUTES

Goods were exchanged along defined routes in First Nations cultures.

There were chains of traders who did business with partners in a neighbouring group. They were usually relations or people who shared the same animal, bird or fish totem.

One of these trade routes ran from the Kimberleys in northwest Australia all the way down to the Eyre Peninsula in South Australia. Along this pathway travelled pearl shells, bamboo necklaces, and boomerangs of a design that was only found in the Kimberleys.

Pearl shells travelled along many trading pathways for hundreds of kilometres across Australia.

Trade items were not just exported out of the Kimberleys. Other items flowed back through the chains of trading partners. Some of these included special spears with bamboo shafts, hooked spears, wooden dishes, dilly bags, ornaments, sacred objects and red ochre.

People in southern Australia were able to get carved pearl shells from the northwest coast or bags of dried pituri from Queensland.

Songs and stories exchanged along these pathways carried with them the wisdom and traditions of many generations, ensuring that knowledge was passed down and shared.

OCHRE

Some trading items were highly valued for a variety of reasons. Ochre was one of these.

Different kinds of ochre had different values placed on it depending on its quality and how important it was for ceremonial use.

The vibrant colours of ochre were used in art and body painting during ceremonies

The red ochre from Parachilna in South Australia was highly prized because of its iridescent quality and deep shade of red. It was considered to be especially sacred and was reserved for use in the most secret ceremonies.

Another important site was at Wilgamia east of Geraldton in Western Australia. To get the ochre from there, the owners had to dig it directly out of the rocks with hardened wooden scrapers. Often, large lumps of rock were taken to an open space and broken up to extract the ochre.

Once the ochre was freed it was pulverised into a powder, dampened with water and kneaded into balls. These were then dried out so that they could be carried and traded.

Ochre, with its vibrant colours, was used in art and body painting during ceremonies, symbolising spiritual and cultural significance.

PITURI

Pituri is a native tobacco plant with a high nicotine content. The leaves have a narcotic effect when chewed.

Pituri

From an area in southwest Queensland, pituri was traded south as far as Lake Eyre, central New South Wales, north Queensland beyond Cloncurry and west beyond Alice Springs into the Central Desert region. Large quantities of pituri used to be traded as far as the Gulf of Carpentaria and to the south around Port Augusta in South Australia.

Pituri was dried, broken into small chips and packaged into specially woven small bags for trading.

First Nations people valued pituri for various reasons. It gave people stamina, enabled them to walk long distances without food and it helped people to talk freely in social situations.

The exchange of pituri not only provided a valuable stimulant but also served as a form of social currency, facilitating meetings and negotiations.

CEREMONIAL GIFTS

Ceremonies transported from one region to another enhanced the spiritual and cultural life of communities, linking them together in a shared cultural landscape.

Ceremonies were traded

Ceremonies

The exchange of gifts was an important part of most First Nations ceremonies. This was not a trade between people who had taken part in the ceremony; it was more like a marked appreciation of their contribution.

Today First Nations people might sometimes be paid in cash for dancing, singing, painting body designs on dancers or for making ritual objects to be used in the ceremony.

In the past they would expect those helping to come and help them when it was their turn to hold a ceremony. They might be given a gift for taking part.

Apart from the ritual exchange of gifts, ceremonies themselves were often traded. They were exported over long distances to people who did not know the language of the songs and who had very little understanding of what the songs and dances were about.

These people, in turn, passed on the ceremony to others in exchange for goods.

People were free to add to or alter the songs and dances once they had been given them. In time, the songs and dances bore little resemblance to the original versions which were retained by the people who first performed them.

There is evidence of women's ceremonies involving love magic travelling from Central Australia up into the Kimberleys and Arnhem Land.

From northeast Australia very important ceremonies were exchanged. For example, a ceremony called *Kunapipi* was passed through Arnhem Land onto Darwin and then south to Katherine and into the Victoria River area of the Northern Territory.

As it was passed from one area to another the people were taught the meaning of its songs and dances.

Dance has rituals

**Ceremonies were often traded and people were taught
the meaning of songs and dances**

Secret sacred ceremonies were not exchanged. These could
only be performed by those people who owned the ceremonies
at the site to which the ceremony belonged.

INTERNATIONAL TRADE

Long before the British occupation of Australia in 1788, possibly for several centuries, there was a trade relationship between First Nations people with people of Southeast Asia and China.

A trade route across the ocean linked the northern shores of Australia to Asia.

By the late seventeenth century, China was looking for fresh sources of trepang. Trepang, also known as *beche-de-mer,* is a sea slug or sea cucumber. It was a valuable product for export and it dominated the trading communities in the Asian region.

Trepang was a prized delicacy in Chinese cuisine. It is elongated in shape with a leathery skin and is found on the bottom of the sea. It is known for its "cure all" medicinal and aphrodisiac qualities and there was a big market for it in China.

Trepang is also recognised as a dietary supplement throughout East Asia and Southeast Asia for treating a range of ailments, such as ulcers, high blood pressure and when made into an ointment it was used for dealing with various skin conditions.

Trepang was the largest Indonesian export to China which was controlled by Chinese merchants living in Macassar which is situated on the southwest peninsular of Sulawesi in Indonesia. It was the centre of a trading network.

It was the Macassans who fished for the trepang.

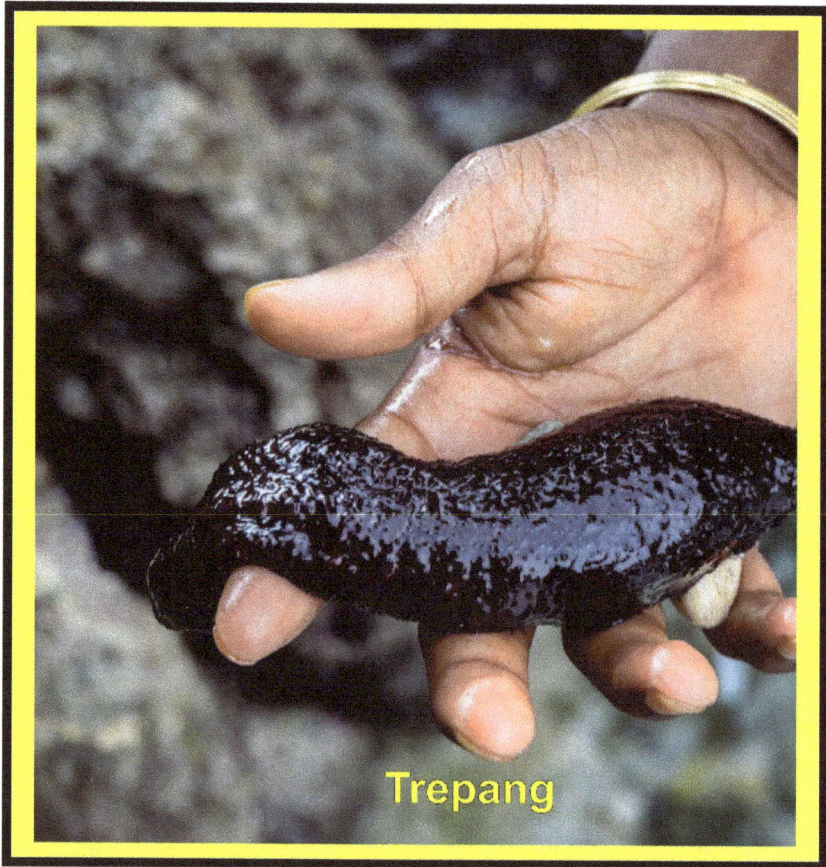

Trepang

Macassans came to the northern Australian coast for a period of several hundred years to just after the conclusion of the nineteenth century. At least a thousand Macassans from the Indonesian island of Sulewesi visited northern Australia each year.

The Macassans would process the trepang on Australia's northern shores for the lucrative Chinese market.

Each year, they would visit Australia. They stayed on the northern shores for approximately five months at a time and then they would head back in April of each year to Macassar when the winds changed to the south-east.

The Macassans established settlements on the sheltered coastline in Arnhem Land not far from the shallow waters where the trepang was collected and they set up processing plants for the trepang.

The remains of Macassan camps can be seen along the northern coast and are usually marked by tamarind trees which grew from seeds left behind by the Macassan visitors.

Tamarind tree

antᵃρ

RELATIONSHIPS WITH FIRST NATIONS PEOPLE

The Macassan traders established close relationships with First Nations people particularly the Yolngu of northeast Arnhem Land. Yolngu people were employed to work collecting and preparing the trepang.

They learnt to communicate with the Macassans. A trade language developed. Yolngu people would travel with the Macassans along the coast, with some even returning with them to spend the dry season in Sulawesi.

A lively trade went on between the Macassans and the local First Nations people. Relations were pretty much friendly with the same boats and fishermen returning each year to the same places.

MACASSAN CULTURAL INFLUENCE

The Yolngu people used turtle shell, pearl shell and cypress timber to exchange for knives, axes, cloth and tobacco.

Shells were traded

It was the Macassans who introduced the smoking of tobacco to coastal First Nations peoples using long Macassan pipes. There was also a regular source of alcohol. Drug substances such as alcohol, tobacco, betel nut and possibly opium were brought on the voyages from Asia.

Macassan words crept into the local language as did tools and the making of the dugout canoe.

Yolngu, knowing the benefits of using the introduced iron tools, began to manufacture dugout canoes for themselves since they were much more stable and seaworthy than the traditional ones made from bark.

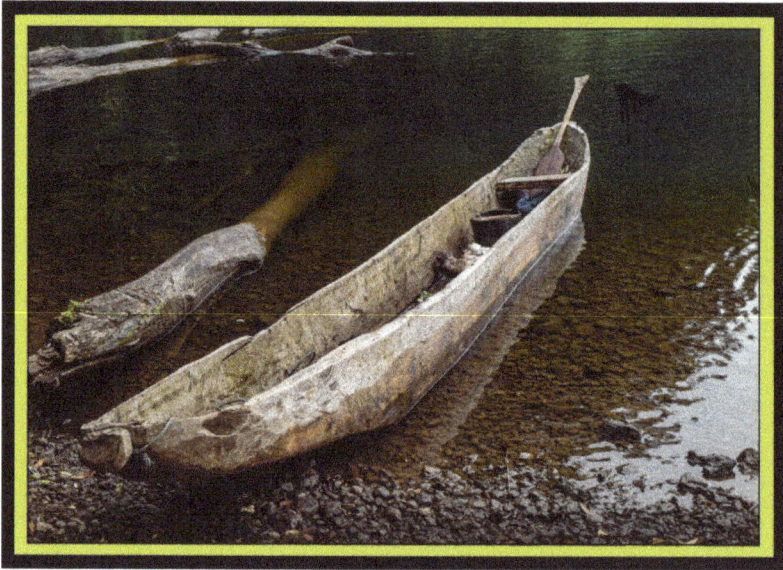

Dugout canoe

They learnt how to work iron from the Macassan traders. Trade with the Macassans would have been one of the main sources of metal for use in shovel-nose spears. This then provided Yolngu with a valuable commodity for trade with other First Nations groups inland.

Macassan influence has been seen in the social, spiritual, symbolic and ceremonial lives of the Yolngu in intricate and complex ways. New technologies and practices were introduced to the local First Nations communities.

This international exchange brought in goods and ideas from afar and allowed First Nations communities to maintain a dynamic interaction with other cultures.

The international trade links with Southeast Asia and China highlight the global connections of Australia's First Nations people.

These connections demonstrate a sophisticated level of maritime navigation and trade expertise that predates European contact. The interactions between Macassan traders and First Nations communities brought not only goods but also new languages, technologies, and practices. All of this enriched the cultural mosaic of Australia First Nations people.

Trade was a central part of life for First Nations people prior to the British settlement of Australia. A flourishing economy existed with trading pathways crisscrossing the continent dispersing goods, information, technologies and culture thousands of kilometres away from their origins.

Trading pathways crisscrossed the continent

Just like the trade and trading routes which existed in other parts of the world, First Nations people had their own. The Australian trading routes connected First Nations people throughout the entire country including the Torres Straits, Papua New Guinea and even internationally with Asia.

Glossary

Aerodynamics The way objects move through air

Pituri A plant also known as *mingkulpa* and is a mixture of leaves and wood ash traditionally chewed as a stimulant by First Nations Australians

Industriousness A personality trait which determines how hardworking, determined, diligent and persistent a person is

Iridescent Showing luminous colours that seem to change when seen from different angles

Ingenuity The skill of being clever in devising something

Sources

The author acknowledges the following sources of information.

Barlow, Alex 1994 *Trade.* South Melbourne, Macmillan Education (Aboriginal Technology)

Berndt, R.M & C.H. 1988 *The World of the First Australians.* Canberra, Aboriginal Studies Press

Blair, Sandy & Hall, Nicholas 2013 "Travelling the 'Malay Road': Recognising the heritage significance of the Macassan maritime trade route" in *Macassan History and Heritage Journeys, Encounters and Influences* Edited by Marshall Clark and Sally K. May   Canberra, ANU E Press https://library.dbca.wa.gov.au/static/FullTextFiles/92478 8.pdf

https://www.odysseytraveller.com/articles/ancient-aboriginal-trade-routes-of-australia/

Low, T. 1987 "Pitjuri: tracing the trade routes of an Indigenous intoxicant" in *Australian Natural History*, 22(6):257-260

Macknight CC. 1976. *The Voyage to Marege: Macassan Trepangers in Northern Australia* Melbourne: Melbourne University Press

Manez, Kathleen Schwerdtner & Ferse, Sebastian C.A. 2010 "The History of Makassan Trepang Fishing and Trade"

PLoS One. 5(6): e11346.
https://www.ncbi.nlm.nih.gov/pmc/articles/PMC2894049

Queensland Museum Indigenous Science. 2012 "Australia had
Ancient Trade Routes Too" https://blog.qm.qld.gov.au/
/05/16/indigenous-science-australia-had-ancient-trade-
routes-too-2/

Who is Marji Hill

Marji Hill, artist and painter since childhood, runs her art career alongside her career as an author.

She is a highly respected international author as well as a seasoned business executive, researcher and coach.

Marji is passionate about promoting understanding between Australia's first people and other Australians.

The spirit of reconciliation was fostered in all her writings ever since she was a Research Fellow in Education at the Australian Institute of Aboriginal and Torres Strait Islander Studies (AIATSIS) in Canberra.

From 2008 to 2011, Marji was Deputy Chairperson of the Mosman Branch of Reconciliation Australia in Sydney.

Following her Research Fellowship at AIATSIS in 1976 Marji, together with her late partner, Alex Barlow, produced more than seventy (70) books on all aspects of the First Nations people including the critical, annotated bibliography *Black Australia*.

In 1989 she was the Project Coordinator and one of the researchers and writers of *Australian Aboriginal Culture* the official Australian Government publication on First Nations people.

In 1988 *Six Australian Battlefields* was published by Angus and Robertson. A decade later it was re-published by Allen & Unwin as a paperback edition.

Her nine-volume encyclopaedia, *Macmillan Encyclopaedia of Australia's Aboriginal Peoples* was published in 2000 and in 2009 she published *The Apology: Saying Sorry to The Stolen Generations.*

Marji's more recent publications extend to self-improvement and self-help with books like *Staying Young Growing Old* and *Inspired by Country* a self-help book about painting with gouache.

More Books by Marji Hill

First Nations

Hill, Marji 2021 *Australian Aboriginal History: 5 Stories of Indigenous Heroes.* Broadbeach, Qld, The Prison Tree Press.

Hill, Marji 2021 *First People Then and Now: Introducing Indigenous Australians.* 2nd ed. Broadbeach, Qld, The Prison Tree Press.

Aboriginal Global Pioneers

Hill, Marji 2024 *Australian Aboriginal Origins: Earliest Beginnings.* Broadbeach, Qld, The Prison Tree Press. (Book 1)

Hill, Marji 2024 *Australian Aboriginal Trade: Sharing Goods and Services.* Broadbeach, Qld, The Prison Tree Press. (Book 2)

Hill, Marji 2024 *Australian Aboriginal Religion: Country and Dreaming.* Broadbeach, Qld, The Prison Tree Press. (Book 3)

Hill, Marji 2024 *Australian Aboriginal Fire: Managing Country.* Broadbeach, Qld, The Prison Tree Press. (Book 4)

Hill, Marji 2024 *Australian Aboriginal Medicine: Caring for People.* Broadbeach, Qld, The Prison Tree Press. (Book 5)

Self-improvement/Self-Help

Hill, Marji 2014 *Staying Young Growing Old.* Broadbeach, Qld, The Prison Tree Press.

Hill, Marji 2020 *How Big Is Your Why? An Author's Guide to Time Management and Productivity to Achieve Transformational Results.* Broadbeach, Qld, The Prison Tree Press.

Hill, Marji 2020 *A Create and Publish Toolbox: 101 Prompts In A Guided Journal To Help You Write, Self-publish, And Market Your Book On Amazon.* Broadbeach, Qld, The Prison Tree Press.

Hill, Marji 2021 *Inspired by Country: An Artist's Journey Back to Nature, Landscape Painting with Gouache.* Broadbeach, Qld, The Prison Tree Press.

Hill, Marji 2024 *Australian Paintings: Artworks by Marji Hill.* Broadbeach, Qld, The Prison Tree Press.

Gold

Hill, Marji 2022 *Gates of Gold: The Discovery of Gold, its Legacy and its Contribution to Australian Identity* Broadbeach, Qld, The Prison Tree Press.

Hill, Marji 2022 *Shadows of Gold: Eureka and the Birth of Australian Democracy.* Broadbeach, Qld, The Prison Tree Press.

Hill, Marji 2022 *Gold and the Chinese: Racism, Riots and Protest on the Australian Goldfields.* Broadbeach, Qld, The Prison Tree Press.

Hill, Marji 2022 *Ghosts of Gold: The Life and Times of Jupiter Mosman.* Broadbeach, Qld, The Prison Tree Press.

Hill, Marji 2022 *Blood Gold: Native Police, Bushrangers & Law and Order on the Goldfields.* Broadbeach, Qld, The Prison Tree Press.

www.ingramcontent.com/pod-product-compliance
Lightning Source LLC
Chambersburg PA
CBHW040254100426
42811CB00011B/1262